Spring
is
Here!

Paul Humphrey and
Alex Ramsay

Illustrated by
Robin Lawrie

5

Spring is here and the leaves
are starting to grow again.

What are these yellow flowers called?

They are daffodils.

10

In spring, daffodils open
in the sunshine.

The birds know that spring
is here.

In spring, birds start collecting twigs to build their nests.

Frogs always lay their eggs in spring.

In spring, fruit trees are covered in blossom.

Lots of lambs are born in
the spring.

23

Are other farm animals born in spring, too?

Yes, they are.

Lots of calves and piglets
are born in spring.

In spring, farmers sow
the seed that will grow
into wheat.

29

How many things can you
remember that happen
in spring?